AF573733

American Textiles and Needlework

SHIELA BETTERTON

Illustrations by S. M. Candler

THE AMERICAN MUSEUM IN BRITAIN

ISBN 0 9504971 3 4

Printed in Great Britain by Butler & Tanner Ltd, Frome and London

Introduction

The first English settlers in the New World relied upon ships from England to supply them with cloth. The Mother Country did little to encourage textile manufacture, hoping instead to create a market for English goods. Yet the skills of cloth making and needlework were not to be readily abandoned.

Needlework was an important economic factor in a colonial woman's life. It was essential for her to know how to prepare yarn and to make and repair clothing and other household textiles. Because of the limitations of early looms there were no patterned fabrics so she had also to know how to make decorative effects with her needle. In the period of early settlement she was too busy providing necessities to do much embroidery, but by the eighteenth century sewing was being taught, often by widows or unmarried women, in schools especially for needlework and embroidery. Professional help with drawing patterns was available by this time, although most women made their own, often copying pictures of birds and flowers from books or from nature. From about 1700 onwards embroidery designs were published in magazines.

Thimbles were a prized possession and a popular gift. They were often made of brass, but ivory, bone and silver were also used. Needles were expensive and had to be imported; a well-to-do woman would keep them in a specially made container. Pins were a luxury. In the eighteenth century they were made from two pieces of wire, the heads being attached to the shaft by hand. It was not until 1831 that John Howe of New York invented a machine for making solid-headed pins.

Pin-cushions holding hand-made pins were often given as presents to an expectant mother or a new baby.

After 1630 many colonists brought sheep with them to America, and colonial legislatures encouraged the growth of flax and the manufacture of linen. At this time all clothes were of wool or linen, cotton not becoming a staple crop until 1760. The importance of these two fibres is obvious from the fact that in 1674 Rhode Island made wool legal tender at twelve pence per pound. Likewise William Penn in 1683 made flax and hemp legal tender in Pennsylvania.

In 1643 twenty families from Yorkshire settled near Ipswich in Massachusets, and started a fulling mill, the first of its kind in America. Their chief product was woollen cloth, though they also used flax. Despite this early example of industrialization, cloth making was largely a cottage industry. All the processes were carried out in the home and turning flax into linen was a lengthy process. It took sixteen months from the time the flax seed was planted to produce the pieces of finished fabric. Wool took nearly as long. Each type of fibre had to be cleaned, wool was carded, flax heckled, then both were spun into yarn, dyed and woven. Children were often given the tasks of carding and heckling and were deft spinners. The small flax wheel was also used for wool but in the mountain areas the great wheel continued to be used for wool into this century. It is said that a woman walked ten miles a day when spinning on the great wheel.

When wool became plentiful a practical and hard wearing material was made from one third white wool, one third black sheep's wool and one third scraps dyed with indigo. This fabric was known as 'Puritan Grey'. Other early fabrics were fustian, a mixture of linen and cotton, and a wool/linen mixture called 'linsey-wolsey'.

Vegetable dyes were used, indigo being principally for blue

and madder for shades of red and brown. Many early textiles were blue, possibly because indigo is a reliable dye, fast and strong enough to cover small discolourations in the fabric.

By the beginning of the eighteenth century the American textile industry was strong enough to cause apprehension amongst English manufacturers. To the skills and knowledge of the English settlers had been added those of the Dutch in New York, the Scots-Irish in New Hampshire, the Swedes in Delaware and the Germans in Pennsylvania. Only in the southern states did the textile industry remain relatively unimportant. From there plantation crops such as tobacco were shipped to England, and in turn English merchandise, including cloth, was purchased through agents in London. Silk was cultivated but was not an important industry at that time. Cotton too was used, and is indigenous to America, although for many years it was imported from Barbados. The importance of cotton, however, belongs to a later period when the invention of the cotton gin revolutionized the industry.

During the eighteenth century the factory system began to develop in England. The policy of the British Government was still aimed at confining the colonists to the production of raw materials and preventing competition with manufacturing interests at home. Every effort was made to keep the developments in textile machinery from spreading to the colonies. It was only a matter of time, however, before the secrets were learnt. Sometimes plans were memorized, as in the case of Samuel Slater, who emigrated from England to America in 1789, and successfully constructed a spinning frame based on Arkwright's invention. American agents occasionally smuggled to France scale models of English machinery, dismantled into small pieces, which were then shipped to America to be re-assembled as patterns for the manufacture of full-scale machinery.

At first American cotton manufacturers found it difficult to compete with the English whose goods were preferred. At the time of the War of Independence, it was considered patriotic to use only cloth which had been made in the colonies, as this old song shows:

> Young ladies in town and those who live 'round,
> Wear none but your own country linen,
> Of economy boast; let your pride be the most
> To wear clothes of your own make and spinnin'.

However, Indian chintzes, imported into America first in English vessels and later as direct imports, were superior to many European textiles. A variety of Indian chintzes and calicoes had reached America before 1700.

Although factory-made goods became increasingly available to the American housewife during the nineteenth century, many of the skills which had been practised for centuries continued to be used. Needlework especially remained important whether in the making or the decoration of clothes, coverlets, rugs and many other household items. The following chapters deal with some aspects of these home crafts in America.

Coverlets

Some of the most striking examples of American needlework are to be seen in the many and varied types of bedcovers.

To many people the words patchwork and quilting are synonymous, but they are two entirely different forms of needlework. A true quilt is a textile sandwich, with a top layer (which may be plain fabric, patchwork, applique, or a combination of both techniques), a bottom layer and a filling in between. Quilting is the pattern in running stitch which holds the layers together and is the last process in the making of a quilt.

PATCHWORK

The reasons for the making of patchwork and applique were obviously repair and economy when textiles were scarce and expensive. In early applique pieces of rich woven fabrics, too precious to throw away, were used as a substitute for embroidery.

It is frequently taken for granted that early American quilts were made of patchwork, but there is no evidence to support this. It is certain that the art of quilting was taken from England by the first colonists, but no mention is made of patchwork in any recorded work. Before the War of Independence calamanco, a fine worsted fabric, was exported from England to America to make the tops of some best quilts. Whole fabric was used, often three widths joined together.

The earliest materials known to have been used for patchwork were the 'painted callicoes' or 'chints' first imported from India in the seventeenth century. These fabrics were used to make the earliest known English patchwork at Levens

Hall near Kendal in Cumbria about 1700. The work consists of a quilt and bed hangings, and so far as is known it is the only patchwork in these materials which still exists. No cotton patchwork of the mid-eighteenth century remains but quilts and bedcovers made after 1780 are comparatively numerous.

Nineteenth-century coverlets were very large and could measure anything from nine to twelve feet square. While four-poster beds remained in fashion a set of furnishings in patchwork, including coverlet, valences and curtains, could be a tremendous undertaking. The whole family helped – children threaded needles and cut patches, boys and men made templates, and women and girls sewed. However several interesting quilts with patchwork tops have been made entirely by men.

In America it was traditional that a girl had twelve quilts in her hope chest when she got married, possibly even thirteen, the thirteenth being the grandest one of all, her Bride's quilt. Although the quilting was not undertaken until she became engaged, she started piecing the tops at an early age. It was usual to start with a 'four patch', just four squares of fabric, two of one colour and two of a contrast, sewn together to make a larger square. Later a girl would make a 'nine patch', five squares of one fabric and four of another. When several squares or 'blocks' had been made they would be sewn together in some attractive way to make the top. It needed an artistic eye to visualize the final result when all the small units had been joined together. Sometimes there would be a pattern in each block, sometimes a block of plain fabric alternated with the pieced block.

The tops of the earliest American quilts were whole cloth, then when India chintzes and calicoes began to be imported tiny scraps were kept and sewn together 'crazy' fashion. Later, when textiles were more easily obtainable a co-ordinated design would be used. Also about this time tops were made by cutting out the floral motifs from worn out furnishings of India chintz and sewing them on to a calico background thus making a new piece of whole fabric. By about 1830 American women could buy American printed cottons, and by 1850 women on the eastern seaboard were able to buy enough fabric by the yard to make some of the more intricate pieced and appliqué patterns. However, the continuing westward expansion meant that frontier conditions were always present and there was always a need for warm bedding. Women therefore continued to meet the challenge of finding new ways of piecing together the scraps of material which they so zealously hoarded.

Most patchwork patterns are geometric, straight lines being easy to sew and more economical of fabric. Certain motifs recur in patchwork, appliqué and quilting in both America and Britain – baskets, pineapples, feathers and stars among many others.

Patterns for pieced quilt tops were taken from every-day objects. Names such as Bear's Paw, Turkey Tracks, Churn Dash and Windmill tell their own story, as does the Rocky Road to California. Historical events also gave their names to patterns – Whig Rose reminding us of political events in the early days of the colonies, and Queen Charlotte's Crown of the last Queen the colonies had before Independence. Other names were taken from events in the Bible and books such as the *Pilgrim's Progress* widely read by the early settlers.

Names changed as the women and their patterns moved westwards. The North Carolina Lily becomes the Prairie Lily west of the Mississippi, and beyond the Rockies, the Mariposa Lily. The Rocky Road to Kansas becomes the Rocky Road to California. An interesting story tells how the pattern 'Orange Peel' came into being. Oranges were very rare in

America at the end of the eighteenth century, so when a lady was invited to a grand dinner in honour of the Marquis de Lafayette and was served with an orange for dessert, she carefully noted the shape of the segments of orange peel and used this as a basis for a new quilt pattern. Sometimes the pattern is called 'Lafayette's Orange Peel'.

Mosaic patchwork, made with very small pieces, was popular in America during the first half of the nineteenth century. Instructions for making 'honeycomb', a type of mosaic patchwork, appear in Godey's Lady Book for February, 1835.

By the second half of the nineteenth century 'crazy' patchwork was very ornate, being made from silks, satins, brocades and velvets, heavily embellished with embroidery stitches. Many crazy quilts were not bedcovers at all, but were used as sofa 'throws'. This medium was popular in both the United States and Britain and many smaller items such as table runners, cushions, chair seats and chair backs were made in this way. In 1855 Godey's Lady Book advertised a 'kit' to make crazy patchwork.

Changing fashions brought about changes in needlework techniques and patchwork became a country craft kept alive by the women in rural areas of both the United States and Britain. It is only in the last decade that patchwork has once more become an art form.

QUILTING

Like patchwork, quilting is a very old form of needlework, coming originally from the east and spreading through the Middle East to Europe and eventually to America.

Early European quilts were purely utilitarian, the stitching being the minimum required to hold the three layers in place. Later women began to use patterns of stitching which developed into some of those in use today.

In mediaeval times quilted jackets were worn under metal armour to prevent chafing, but light troops had to be satisfied with only a quilted jacket. In seventeenth-century Virginia quilted armour was commonplace. In the seventeenth and eighteenth centuries much clothing was quilted for warmth. In both America and Britain women wore quilted petticoats, the top of silk or calamanco, with a homespun backing and a sheep's wool padding. This dictated a new form of dress, where the skirt was cut away to show the delicate stitching on the quilted petticoat. Men wore quilted breeches and waistcoats and sometimes wooden chests were lined with quilted fabric.

Women from Britain and parts of Europe took with them to America their knowledge of quilting, and up to the time of the Revolution American and British 'best' quilts were very similar. The early quilts had a filling of carded sheep's wool, which by the end of the eighteenth century was superseded by cotton in America. Now modern polyester fabrics are used for padding.

The edges of early quilts were finished by turning in the top and backing and sewing them together with two rows of running stitch, a practice which has remained common in Britain. In addition in America the edges were often bound with hand-loomed tape or, when material was available, with narrow bias strips of fabric.

As time went on American quilts were invariably of pieced or appliqué design and 'best' quilts were often very elaborate. The quilting then became simpler, often in straight lines with the design itself outlined in running stitch. The traditional plain quilt continued to be made in England and Wales.

The quilting frame was a familiar sight in many homes and usually rested on four straight-backed chairs which were kept for this purpose. The quilt backing was sewn lengthwise into

1. *The quilting frame was once a familiar sight in an American home.*

the frame, the filling and top spread on and all three layers tacked together. The work was then rolled up on one rail leaving out about 24 inches. When this had been sewn it was rolled under and a fresh part exposed. In eastern Kentucky and eastern Tennessee a full-sized frame was, and still is used. This has a rope at each corner so that when quilting is over for the day the frame can be hauled up to the ceiling out of the way.

Patterns are marked with a yarn needle, or tailor's chalk for dark fabrics, around templates made out of card or tin or plywood. In America many women use lead pencil for marking but this leaves a dirty line which never really washes out. An expert quilter will mark only the outside lines of a design, the rest she will sew in freehand.

Quilting bees were welcome social occasions in both Great Britain and Northern Ireland, but it is with nineteenth-century America that they are usually associated. The women sat round the quilting frame, and while sewing, gossiped and exchanged news. At dusk the frame was put away, and the men joined them for supper. The pleasure felt in these gatherings is recorded in many poems and songs of the time: one of them is 'The Quilting Party' by Stephen Collins Foster:

> In the sky the bright stars gathered
> On the banks the pale moon shone,
> And 'twas from Aunt Dinah's quilting party
> I was seeing Nellie home.

Public quilting bees were, and still are held, for example the women members of a church gathering to quilt in aid of church funds or some other worthwhile cause.

The two main quilting areas in this country are Northumberland and Durham, and the valleys of South Wales. As a rule the geometric patterns originated in South Wales, while

2. *Traditional quilting patterns.*

those from the north are curved and flowing. Although patterns from these areas have regional characteristics they have spread throughout America and the flowing feather patterns from the north of England can be found as far apart as Maryland and Ohio. Other patterns common to both British and American quilts are the several versions of the rope or chain pattern; the wineglass or teacup; the rose or whorl; and the diamond or cross bar as it is called in America.

Many patterns were taken from homely, commonplace objects and women who lived by the sea might use patterns to represent waves, seaweed or shells, whilst a woman who lived in the country might use feathers, corn, or flowers and leaves. Other patterns had a deeper meaning. The pomegranate symbolized fruitfulness, the pineapple hospitality, the clematis and grapes prosperity and plenty. It was considered unlucky to put hearts on anything but a marriage quilt.

Much quilting in America today is done on the sewing machine but there are dedicated groups of women, particularly some of the church groups, who hand quilt in the traditional way using the traditional patterns.

SOME TYPES OF COVERLETS

All White

It was not until the first half of the nineteenth century that all-white coverlets became popular in the United States of America. They were made for decorative purposes rather than warmth and were very suited to the Greek Revival and Empire styles of furnishings. The making of an all-white quilt, where the attractiveness depended solely on the design, presented a far greater challenge to the needlewoman than the making of a patchwork one.

The designs tended to be similar, having a basket or vase of flowers in the centre, with fruit and floral and leaf motifs in the four corners.

Although called quilts these bedcovers consisted of only two layers of fabric which were joined together over much of the surface with small running stitches. Other techniques used were Italian quilting (drawing a cord or 'roving' between two parallel rows of running stitch to raise the surface) and Trapunto or 'stuffed work'. Here a tiny hole was made in the backing and scraps of cotton were pushed through until the surface of the work was sufficiently raised. The edges of the hole were then caught together with neat stitches. This was a technique used very effectively for grapes, stars, and the buds of floral motifs.

Other types of all-white bedcovers used a cotton 'roving' (an inexpensive type of twisted cotton, similar to that used for making the wicks of candles) for embroidery or as part of the woven pattern.

Some spreads made of linen or cotton twill were embroidered with a design in a light-weight 'roving', a heavier cord being used for the laid and couched work. The couching was not drawn through the cloth but was formed into a braid which was then sewn on to the surface of the work. This type of embroidery stemmed from the seventeenth- and early eighteenth-century English work where bedspreads of twilled linen were embroidered with a fine white cord, laid and couched.

Candlewicking was also used in woven spreads which had a fine white cotton warp and weft. The raised pattern was made by the weaver picking up with a piece of stick or wire certain loops of the roving from the flat weaving. The loops could be cut if a fluffy effect was desired.

The patterns used for woven candlewick spreads were often

3. *Some appliqué border designs.*

4. *This Presentation Quilt from the Museum collection, with its appliqué* [illegible]

geometric sometimes resembling those patterns of patchwork quilts.

Album Quilts

An album quilt was a co-operative effort. Each of the many squares was made by a different individual or group who wished to honour the person to whom the quilt was to be presented. The squares, signed by the makers and often dated, included motifs relevant to the recipient's life or interests. Scripture quilts included passages from the Bible written on fabric which was then sewn on to the block. Bride's quilts always included hearts. A Friendship quilt was often made by members of a church and presented to one of its members or to the minister. A Freedom quilt would be made for a young man by the girls of his acquaintance on his reaching the age of twenty-one. It would then be put away until he gave it as his gift to the hope chest of his future bride. Between the years 1842 and 1852 many quilts with similar patterns were made in the Baltimore area, particularly Bride's quilts, and it is possible that some of the blocks were made from a professionally drawn pattern or were bought in 'kit' form.

Album quilts were also made for hospital use. Weldon's *Practical Patchwork* published about 1900, tells us that 'Hospital quilts are made of good sized squares of red twill and white calico placed alternately like squares on a chess board, the white pieces having texts written on them or scripture pictures outlined in marking ink; they are much appreciated and prove a great source of interest to the poor invalids.'

The indelible ink used was made from powdered galls, green vitriol, gum arabic and alum.

Hawaiian Quilts

Before woven cloth was introduced into the Hawaiian Islands clothes were made from 'tapa', a kind of pounded bark which was felted into the correct shape and needed no sewing. The wives of the New England missionaries brought their scrap bags with them to the islands and taught the native women how to sew and to make patchwork. It is not known just when the traditional patchwork patterns were superseded by the 'all over' appliqué patterns used today. These quilts are made of whole cloth of only two colours using a folded paper 'cut out' technique. The border, 'maile lei', is made in the same way. Patterns are symbolic and recur frequently in different combinations.

The stitching on the Hawaiian quilt follows the line of the applique at half inch intervals so earning the name of 'contour quilting' as it resembles the contour lines on a map.

Pennsylvania German

Patterns on quilts made by the Pennsylvania German women are different from those made in other parts of the American continent. Settlers from Germany and eastern Europe brought with them a peasant love of strong colour, as well as patterns which can be traced back to a mediaeval mid-European culture. They set their own cultural standards, but because of lack of time and money tended to simplify designs and adapt them to American materials. As a consequence they have a distinct character of their own. From the time the tulip was introduced into Europe from the East in the middle of the sixteenth century it became a favourite flower. The tulip shape is used in many Pennsylvania German patterns, both patchwork and quilting. The pattern has a simple outline which even an inexperienced needlewoman could manage.

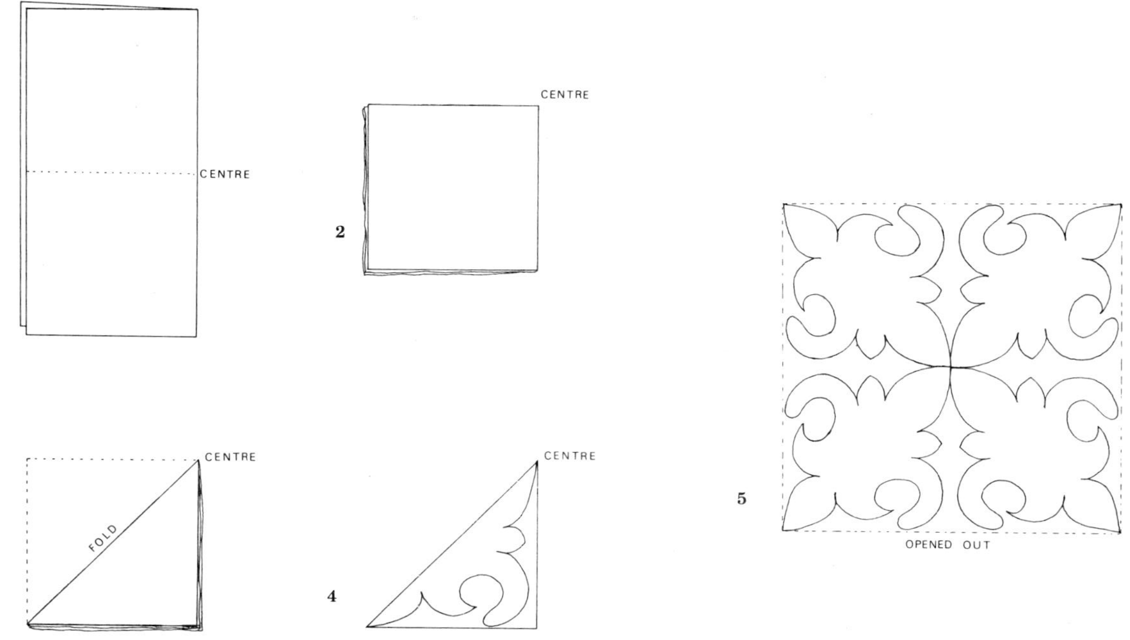

5. *Steps in making Hawaiian Appliqué.*

Many Pennsylvania German quilts show a pattern of a vase of flowers, often in conjunction with birds or animals, patterns which have been known in Europe from the Renaissance onwards.

Some of the finest Pennsylvania German quilts were made during the first half of the nineteenth century.

Amish Quilts

The Amish or Plain People belong to the most conservative section of the Mennonite Church, and of particular interest are the quilts made by the Amish people in Pennsylvania, Indiana, Ohio and Iowa. The Old Order Amish are very strict and almost all forms of decoration are prohibited. As quilts are utilitarian objects, however, colour was allowed although it was essential that the fabrics were of solid colours, no patterned fabrics being allowed. The quilts are usually made of woollen cloth in the same dark sombre colours as the clothing worn by the community, always with a small piece of brilliant contrast fabric.

Patterns were simple and non-representative and always geometric, using variations of the diamond, square and triangle.

Very striking are the Amish 'Bars' quilts. They consist of wide bands of contrasting colours framed in a wide border with squares of a third colour in each corner. Bold contrasts and unusual colour schemes, together with very fine stitching, are a feature of this type of quilt.

Indian Quilts

The Indian women of the Great Plains had no tradition of sewing with needle and thread and only learnt new techniques through contact with white women. Quilts made by Indian women show astonishing colour combinations and the patterns incline to the angular and geometric. However these bold Indian type colours and designs are very much in demand since they combine very happily with modern furniture and decoration.

To Make Patchwork

GENERAL

The materials used should be firm and non-stretch, and fabrics of different strengths should not be used in the same piece of work. Material which is well worn should be avoided, and if old and new fabrics are to be used, the new should be washed first of all to prevent shrinking.

The size of the finished article and the thickness of the material should be taken into account when deciding on the size of the individual patches. Colours and texture should of course be balanced. Stitches are not meant to be invisible, but should not be too obvious. Fine cotton or sewing silk, and as fine a needle as possible, should be used.

In English patchwork pieces of fabric are tacked over a paper shape cut from a template, the resulting patches then being oversewn together on the wrong side. In America, however, the template is placed on the wrong side of the material and marked round with a pencil line. Each shape is then cut out, leaving about one quarter inch fabric for a turning. The shapes are then placed right sides facing, and sewn together along the pencilled line with a running stitch. The seams are all pressed one way.

Three of the simplest motifs are as follows:

HEXAGONAL MOTIFS

(a) In order to achieve a crisp outline and neat angles, hexagons are best made using a template and papers. Templates should be accurate and made of metal or plastic.

(b) Cut one shape for each patch from good-quality paper, using the template as a guide (see illustration 6 figure 1). If

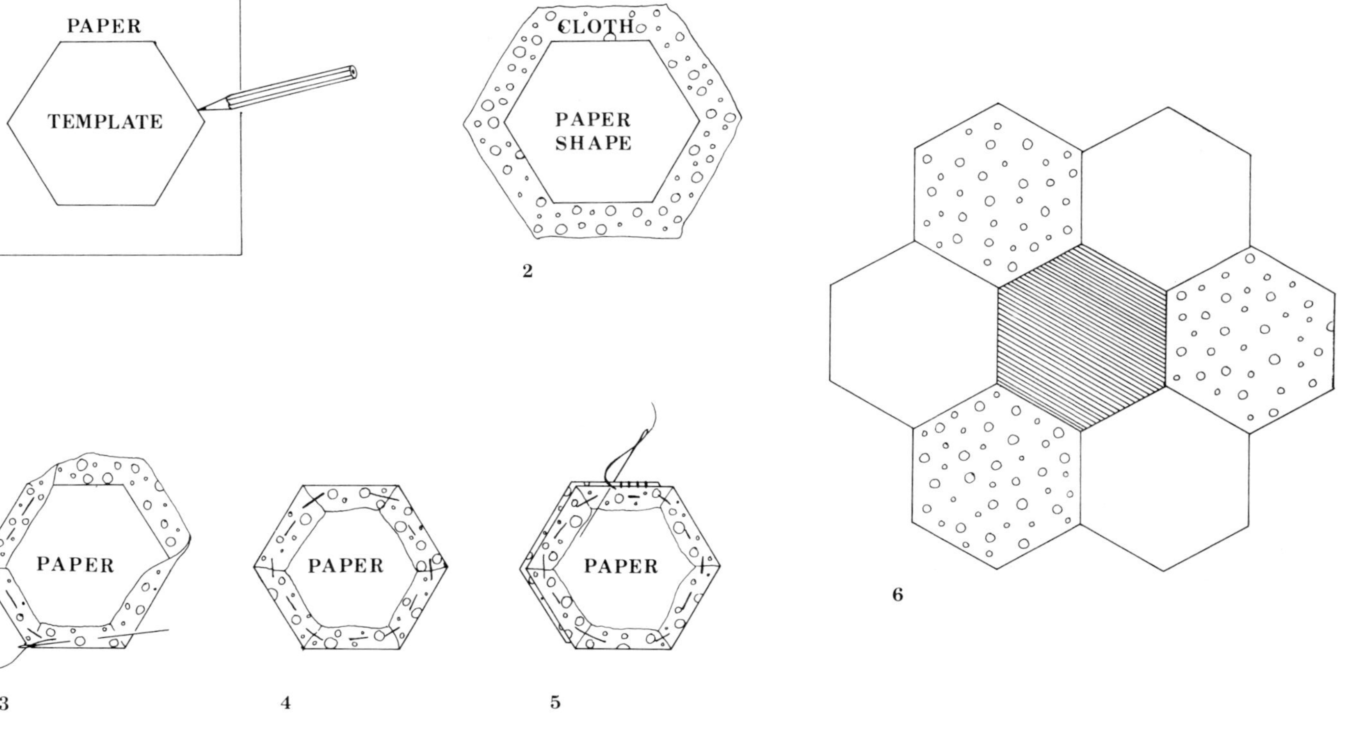

6. *Steps in making a patchwork motif.*

the papers are not cut accurately the completed patchwork will not be flat.

(c) To make the patches place the paper on the reverse side of the material, and cut round, leaving about one quarter inch turning (see illustration 6 figure 2). Fold the turning over firmly and tack round, taking care not to catch the paper (see illustration 6 figures 3 and 4).

(d) Put two patches together, right sides facing and oversew along one side (see illustration 6 figure 5). Patches should meet at the corners if carefully matched.

(e) Sew the patches into units (see illustration 6 figure 6). Then join units together until the required size is reached.

(f) When making the Grandmother's Flower Garden pattern each motif is surrounded with a ring of patches in white or a pastel colour before being joined to the next unit.

NINE PATCH

The completed block is six inches square.

(a) Find two pieces of fabric which look well together.

(b) From cardboard cut out a two inch square.

(c) Place the square cardboard template on the wrong side of the fabric and mark round it with a sharp pencil (illustration 7, figure 1).

(d) Leaving a quarter inch turning all round, cut five squares from one fabric and four from the other.

(e) Arrange squares as shown in illustration 7, figure 2.

(f) With right sides facing sew pieces (a) and (b) together using a running stitch, then join on piece (c). Press seams in the same direction. Do not press seams open.

(g) Join sections two and three in the same way.

(h) Join the three sections together.

(i) Make several blocks in this way then join them together

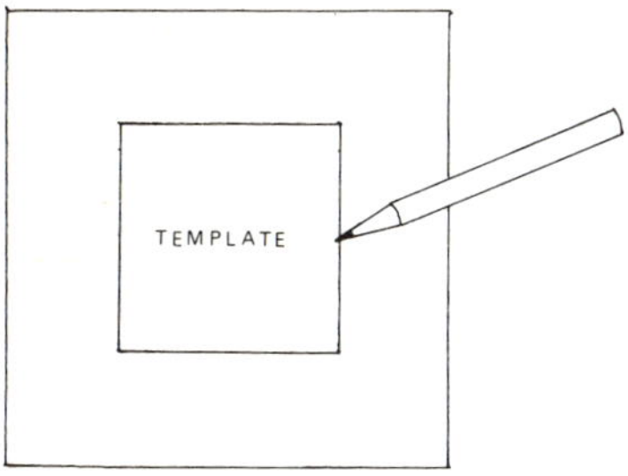

TEMPLATE

FIG.1

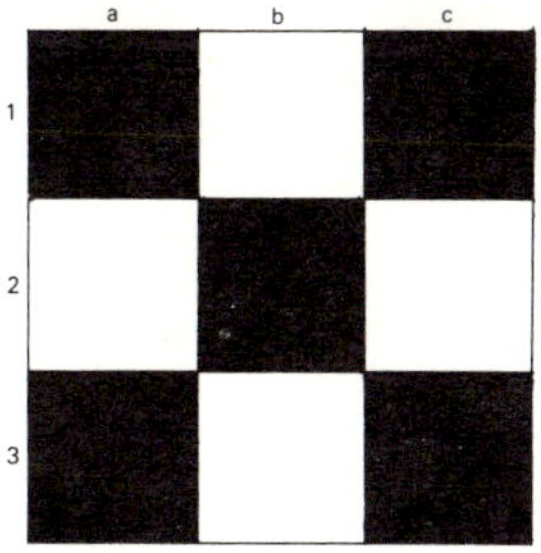

a b c

1

2

3

FIG. 2

FIG. 3

SOLID
COLOUR

FIG. 4

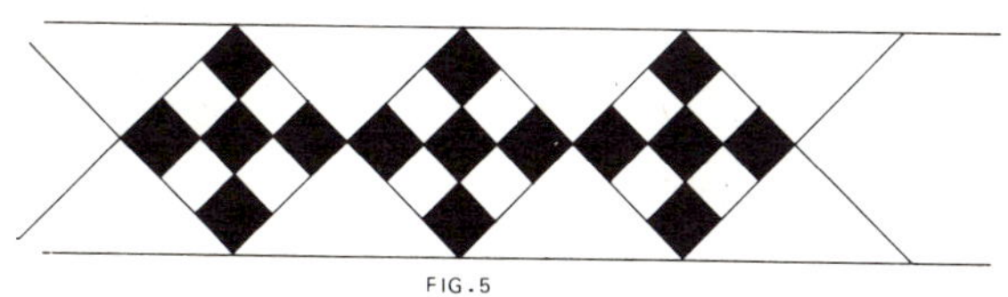

FIG. 5

7. *Steps in making a 'Nine Patch' block.*

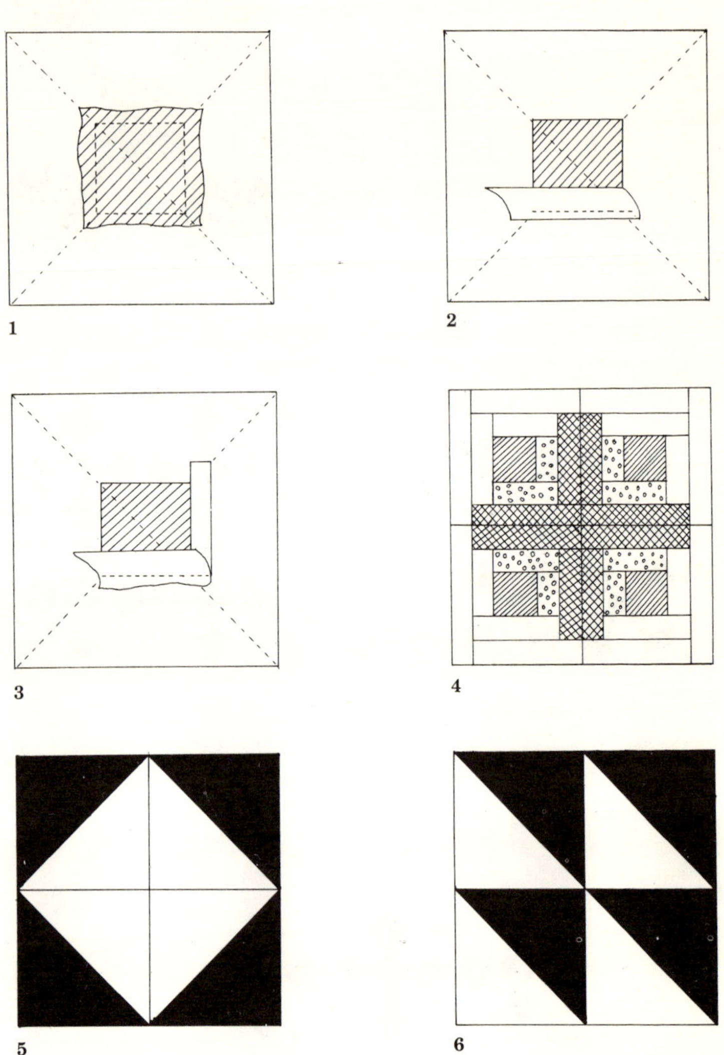

8. *Steps in making a 'Log Cabin' block.*

to make an attractive design. Some suggestions are given in illustration 7, figures 3, 4 and 5.

LOG CABIN

The completed block is 9 inches square.

(a) Cut a piece of foundation fabric 10 inches square.

(b) Crease diagonally each way.

(c) Assemble five different fabrics in light shades and five in dark shades, also a three-inch square of contrast fabric.

(d) Tack the three-inch square exactly in the centre of the foundation block (illustration 8, figure 1).

(e) Cut two strips of light material and two of dark about two inches longer than the central square.

(f) With right sides facing and edges matching sew the first light strip to the central square using a running stitch one quarter of an inch in from the edge through to the foundation block. Fold away from the centre (illustration 8, figure 2).

(g) Repeat with second light strip and then the two dark strips on the other three sides (illustration 8, figure 3).

(h) Repeat process with other fabrics making the strips longer on each row and keeping light and dark fabrics always at the same side. The crease on the foundation block shows where the strips should interlock.

(i) Some ways of joining the blocks together are shown in illustration 8, figures 4, 5 and 6.

Woven Coverlets

Despite the very early establishment of the textile factory at Rowley in Massachusetts, weaving remained largely a cottage industry until after the War of Independence. The need to develop the textile industry was, however, fully appreciated when the delegates from several counties met at Philadelphia on 23rd January 1775 and presented the following resolution to the Provincial Convention:

'That as it was necessary to lay a restraint on importation and supply of articles for subsistence and clothing, and defence must be provided, no person should use, sell or kill for market any sheep under four years old, and it was recommended that woollen manufactories be set up, especially for coating, flannel, blankets, rugs, coverlets, hosiery and coarse cloths.'

Also 'That societies be established and premiums be granted in the several counties to persons who may excel in the several branches of manufacturing.'

However, at a time when warm bedcovers were a necessity and manufactured goods not easily available, most women made their own coverlets, whether woven, tufted or quilted.

The oldest woven bedcovers had a homespun linen warp and the flax went through many processes before it became linen thread. One such process was 'scutching' where the tough outer bark of the flax plant was removed from the line fibre. Scutching was hard work so neighbours helped each other at a 'flax scutching' which was held from time to time. This was a gathering rather like a quilting bee. After the flax had been dealt with there was a supper and dancing and other amusements running far into the night. Although some girls scutched well they were invited mainly to make the gathering attractive to the men who did the scutching. Later the warp was made of locally grown cotton, but that too needed patience and hard work to transform the cotton boll into a fine spun thread, particularly as the early home-made cotton gins were primitive affairs, rather like small clothes wringers.

At first both high and low spinning wheels were used, but gradually the low flax wheel was adapted for use with wool also. On early looms the shuttle was thrown by hand, so early coverlets were made from two or even three narrow widths carefully joined together.

All women were taught to weave simple patterns in the home. For the more complicated patterns, however, the home weaver usually needed skilled assistance. The patterns, called 'drafts', were narrow strips of paper recording a series of straight lines, dots and dashes – the codes by which the design was woven. The drafts were kept rolled and were tied traditionally with black thread.

The simple overshot weave was most generally used and due to the limitations of the loom patterns were always geometric. After 1820 when the Jacquard attachment reached America much more elaborate patterns could be woven. Jacquard's invention, which used a punched card system, enabled groups of warp threads to be raised. The punched cards were held on a continuous roll above the loom, and some of the wires on a block inside the mechanism were depressed according to the position of the holes in the card. The wires were attached to weighted strings which caused the correct group of warp threads forming the pattern to be selected. Also about this time large numbers of skilled weavers emigrated from Scandinavia, Germany and Scotland. After working in the east for some time many moved further west, particularly to Ohio, Indiana, Illinois and Iowa. These Jacquard weavers were professionals and the weaver would incorporate his name or initials, the date, often the name of a town, and sometimes the name of the person for whom the coverlet had been woven, into his piece of work.

For about one hundred years from the 1720's the double weave was popular, particularly in Pennsylvania, where settlers from Scandinavia and Germany had brought patterns with them. As double weave coverlets have two sets of warp threads and two wefts joined at intervals they used a great deal of yarn and were slow to weave so were rarely to be found in the more remote regions.

The term 'summer and winter' weave, used for a certain type of pattern, seems to be a term known only in America. A mixture of dark and light threads have a patterning weft thread floated over and under the structural weave. The explanation of the name 'summer and winter' would seem to be that the light side of the coverlet would be used uppermost during the summer months while the dark side would be used during the winter. The patterns used for this weave are very similar to those used for the overshot.

The names given to coverlet patterns are as wide and varied as those given to quilts, and in many instances one name may be used for both a woven coverlet and a quilt. Historical events gave their names to patterns such as 'Lee's Surrender', and 'Braddock's Defeat'. The 'Whig Rose' probably commemmorates the foundation of the Whig Party in Andrew Jackson's administration. Some names have regional origins as in 'Virginia Barley', and 'Tennessee Trouble', while other names are more prosaic – 'Doors and Windows' or 'Hen Scratch'. Nature has always provided pattern names: 'Flowers of Edinboro' proclaiming its country of origin: 'Dogwood Blossom' and 'Rose in the Wilderness'.

The 'Chariot Wheel', a circle with two diameters crossing

each other at right angles, is one of the oldest designs. In the pictographs of the Moqui Indians of Arizona the symbol for the word 'star' is the hub and spokes of the chariot wheel. The 'Quincunx', five squares or figures, one in the centre and one at each corner, is a frequent feature of coverlet drafts.

The early coverlets were of no more than three colours, natural, indigo dyed blue and reds made from madder dyes.

The great years of coverlet weaving ended with the Civil War, when factory made blankets became cheap and plentiful.

Stencilled Coverlets

At the beginning of the nineteenth century many New England homes had stencilled walls and floors, and by about 1825 coverlets were also being stencilled. Occasionally these coverlets were backed and padded, then quilted.

Stencilled coverlets were made mainly in New England and New York and were probably a development from the theorem paintings on velvet, a craft which was taught in many seminaries for young ladies. Early in the nineteenth century advertisements appeared which offered to teach decorating on cloth as being a faster means of ornamentation then hand embroidery, and from about 1835 stencils could be purchased from a professional cutter. Such spreads were never made commercially.

The design to be stencilled was traced on to oiled paper, tin, or even wood, and a separate stencil was cut for each colour. Early patterns were made up of many units which could be arranged to give a variety of styles. Later stencils were simplified so that a flower for instance would be painted from a single unit. These later stencils do not show the variations of the earlier ones. The method of working involved placing a spread of inexpensive cotton on a flat, slightly padded surface and a plan of the design was marked on the cloth.

Two types of colours were employed. The first method used a concentrated vegetable dye mixed with gum arabic so that it would not run. This colour was difficult to set, however, and began fading immediately it was applied. The second method employed a ground-up pigment in oil, bought from a hardware store. It was mixed with a substance called 'stencil mordant' which set the colours more permanently. The paint was tamped through the stencils, one colour at a time, sometimes with a brush or with a pad of cloth. To give more detail some parts of the pattern were touched up freehand after the stencil had been removed.

Bed Rugs

The word 'rug' is derived from the Scandinavian RYIJS meaning 'a rough material'. In Britain the word 'rug', sometimes spelt 'rugg', meant a warm bedcover, but there was little to distinguish these rugs from blankets, and no evidence has been found that they were needlework rather than woven.

In the will of John Smith, Clothier, of Bradford on Avon, Wiltshire, made in 1666, he left among other effects 'one green rugg, one pair blancotts, and one red coverlid'. An Inventory of Goods of William Trent, New Jersey in 1726 includes 'Feather beds, bolsters, blankets, ruggs and quilts to the value of £38 9s.'

Colonists brought rugs to America and they were also imported from France and Spain. They were made of wool and of one colour, commonly green, and may have been placed at the foot of the bed, perhaps folded, to be used when resting during the day as well as at night. However, about 1720 a different type of bed rug, which seems to have originated in Connecticut, appeared, and these were made and used for almost a century.

These decorative bed rugs, which were treasured possessions, were meant to be seen and would be the topmost cover of the bed. They were large and reached to the floor on three sides, the two lower corners being rounded. Unlike some types of floor rugs these bed rugs were not made from left over fabrics, but the complete design was worked out in advance and made at home from home-produced yarn. The base was of wool, linen or linsey wolsey, and the entire ground fabric was covered with embroidery. A large needle made of wood, bone or even whalebone, threaded with as many as nine or ten strands of yarn, was used to sew with a running stitch, often over a reed which raised loops on the surface. These could be cut to form a pile or left uncut. Many examples had a fringe round three sides.

Blue was the most common colour and it was used with great effect in conjunction with browns or natural shades. Greens and reds were very sparingly used.

The patterns were not native to America but probably derived from the English designed, Indian made palampores (chintz bed covers). Another source of design may have been the block printed papers used to line chests and document boxes which were known to have inspired embroidery designs during the seventeenth century. The patterns all show a marked similarity. A large flowering plant fills the centre and it is surrounded with a curving vine with flowers or leaves in each curve.

Floor Coverings

In the early colonial period floors were of bare earth. Later they were boarded and sanded, the sand often being swept into a pattern. By the middle of the eighteenth century floors and canvases were being painted to represent woven carpets, tile pavements or parquet, in imitation of some of the floor treatments in English houses of the period. Before long, however, canvas floor cloths became accepted on their own merits and were made professionally as well as by thrifty housewives in their own homes.

Carpets were originally covers for tables and in old inventories there is often doubt as to whether the carpet is meant as a floor covering or a furniture covering. In 1798, an encyclopaedia published in Philadelphia defined a carpet as 'a sort of covering of stuff, or other materials, wrought with the needle or on a loom, which is part of the furniture of a house and commonly spread over tables or laid upon the floor'.

After 1725 Oriental carpets gradually began to appear in well-to-do homes, followed by the importation of British carpets made on hand looms operated by organized groups of professional weavers. By the middle of the century carpets were being used on both tables and floors, at which time they acquired special uses such as entry, floor, table, or bedside carpet.

The first imported carpets came by way of Turkey and thus, regardless of place of origin, were always known as Turkish. Herat rugs were brought into Europe in great quantities during the seventeenth century and a few were believed to have found their way to America. By 1770 eastern carpets were being used on the floor.

By the middle of the eighteenth century carpet making had become a well-established industry in England and Scotland, and British-made goods were popular in the American home, Wiltons and Axminsters being advertised in New England before the Revolution. A carpet factory at Loxley's Court, owned by William Calverly, was first mentioned in 1774, and it was said that his carpets were better than the imported kind. In 1791 a William Sprague started a factory in Philadelphia. In 1816 Alexander Hamilton put a small duty on foreign carpeting – the first tariff imposed to protect American made carpets. By 1830 the American carpet industry was well under way, although until the time of the Civil War the inexpensive two-ply ingrain was almost the only carpeting made in quantity.

YARN SEWN RUGS

These were made in America during the eighteenth century and at the beginning of the nineteenth century. They were rectangular in shape and were mainly made to cover chests and tables and not to put upon floors. The base was usually homespun linen and the design was filled in with a continuous running stitch. Loops were left on the surface which could be cut to form a pile if desired. The back of the rug shows small stitches with a great deal of the base material showing in between.

TONGUE RUGS

Here a strong cloth was used, pieces of thick warm material being sewn to it, each piece overlapping the previous one rather like tiles on a roof.

BUTTON RUGS

Strong cloth such as sail cloth was used as a base. Three circles of woollen cloth decreasing in size were sewn one on top of the other, the smallest at the top. The whole 'button' was then sewn on to the base. Sometimes the 'buttons' were decorated with embroidery stitches.

SHIRRED RUGS

Shirred rugs are often called 'chenille' rugs from the French word meaning caterpillar, and most of them were made before the Civil War. Strips of cloth were cut and a thread taken down the middle with running stitch. The thread was then drawn up to give a shirred effect and the result looked rather like a caterpillar. Each piece was then applied to a linen or tow backing. The reverse shows nothing except the stitches which secure the surface fabric 'caterpillar' to the backing.

BRAIDED RUGS

Made chiefly at the end of the nineteenth century, braided rugs used materials such as serge or gaberdine which are not suitable for hooking. Strips of material two inches in width, had the edges turned in to make a one-inch strand. These strands were grouped in threes, fives or sevens, and plaited to make the braid. Braided rugs were always round or oval. The end of the braid is turned in on itself and firmly stitched. The braid is then wound round this core and sewn at intervals until the required size and shape is reached.

RAG RUGS

Rag rugs were woven, and were an easy and economical way of using up left over cotton and linen materials. The warp was a strong linen or cotton thread and the cotton and linen fabrics were torn into strips and used as weft.

HOOKED RUGS

During the nineteenth century hooked rugs were the most widely used floor rugs, the earliest example dating from the

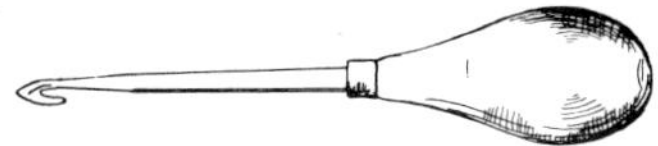

HOOKED

CROSS SECTION

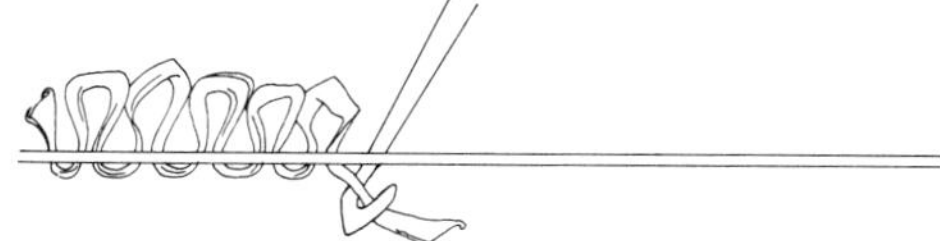

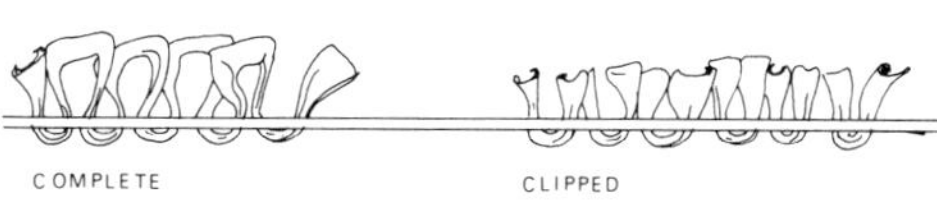

REVERSE

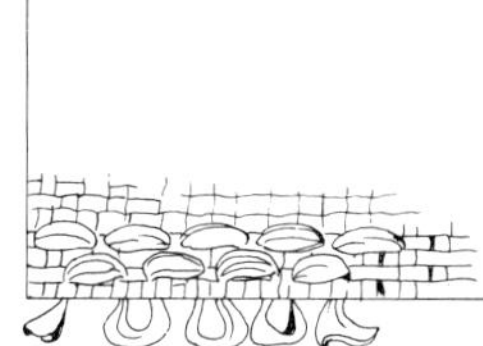

YARN SEWN

CROSS SECTION

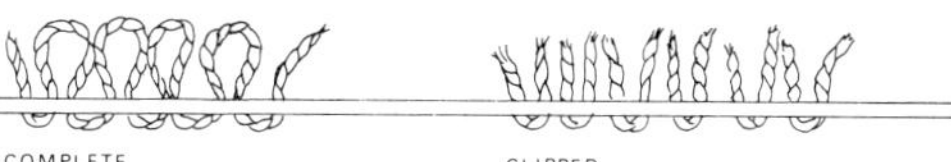

REVERSE

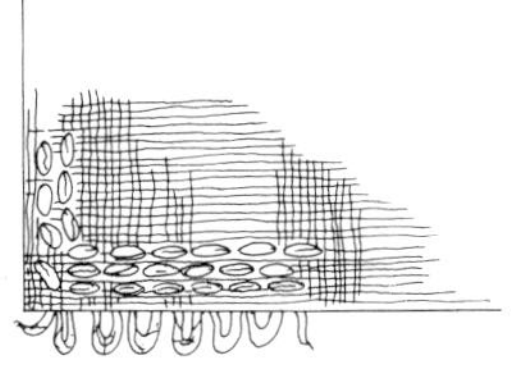

9. *Hooked and Yarn Sewn Rugs.*

10. *Two hooked rugs from the Museum collection.*

1830's. This type of floor covering had been known in Egypt, Scandinavia and Britain, and sailors had made rope 'sennits' using the same technique.

Early rugs were worked on a linen foundation. About 1850 jute began to be imported into America, and burlap, which is a derivative of jute, superseded linen as a base fabric. A strip of cloth between one-sixteenth and one-quarter inch wide was pulled from the underside through the foundation, leaving on top a series of loops about half-an-inch high. These formed the pile which could be cut for a softer effect. This is the type of rug which is also made in parts of Britain but with wider strips of fabric. The hook, rather like a coarse crochet hook, often with a wooden handle, could be made from a large nail, skewer or carpet needle. By the end of the nineteenth century specially manufactured hooks were available.

An American housewife might have made two rugs of average size each winter. Many varied and intricate designs were used. In the New England coastal towns whaling scenes and seascapes were popular, while inland landscapes and pictures of houses and animals were more common. Floral designs similar to those used in Aubusson and Savonnerie carpets appeared among the French settlers in Quebec and Nova Scotia and were copied in the United States.

Neutral colours came from practical hard-wearing clothes and red from flannel underwear. However many women made use of the newly discovered aniline dyes to achieve the special shades which they needed for their patterns.

Probably more hooked rugs were made in the last quarter of the nineteenth century than at any other time. This was largely due to the efforts of one man, Edward Sands Frost of Biddeford, Maine, who was invalided out of the army and became a pedlar. He added rug patterns designed by himself to the usual pedlar's stock. He also sold burlap on which the patterns were already marked and used metal stencils as a quick method of marking the patterns and indicating the colours. Frost continued to peddle his rug designs until the beginning of the twentieth century. By this time rug making, like many other skills, had spread westwards with the pioneers into many parts of the American continent.

Crewel Embroidery

Crewel is a worsted yarn of two threads, not the stitches nor the patterns which are often given the same name and which were developed in the nineteenth century. Worsted yarns had been used for embroidery in many European countries but the crewel embroidery of America stems directly from that worked in England during the seventeenth and eighteenth centuries.

Most American crewel embroidery was done in New England and at first had a strong English influence, particularly in the Boston area. Gradually the knowledge of this type of work spread and by the mid-eighteenth century the artistic lead had been taken by Connecticut.

The settlers looked to England both for goods and traditions. Advertisements in newspapers of the day, as well as the quality of the materials used, indicate that both background fabrics and crewel yarns were usually imported from England. Jacobean bedhangings of the seventeenth and eighteenth centuries were sold as kits in England and America – the pattern was already drawn on to the fabric. Steel needles which were being manufactured in England by the seventeenth century also encouraged this new interest in embroidery.

During the early colonial period the principal bed was always in the parlour, and beautifully embroidered crewel-work bed hangings showed off the needlewoman's skill. Coverlet, headcloth, valences, and side curtains would all be of crewel work. There is no evidence to suggest that crewel embroidery was ever used to decorate window curtains. This type of embroidery was also used for chair seats, and various items of clothing such as petticoats and aprons, as well as for

11. *Crewel work designs.*

smaller articles such as pocket books, pockets and polescreens. By the end of the eighteenth century and on into the early nineteenth century home-woven blankets were being embroidered with crewel yarns.

The form a coverlet would take was largely determined by the width of the loom on which the ground fabric was woven. If the loom was narrow the coverlet would be of two or three widths joined together. If there was a centre seam the tree of life or a large flowering plant or basket of flowers and fruit sometimes disguised the join. There was often no attempt to hide the join, and patterns of trailing vines ascended up each breadth. Other coverlets ignored the joins completely, and the whole surface was embroidered with clusters of flowers and foliage.

Although chain stitch was used a great deal in early styles, the two most popular stitches in American crewel work were Roumanian Couching (also known as New England laid stitch) and flat stitch. Also used were outline and ladder stitches with french knots, bullion and seed stitches for special effects. Seldom were there more than four or five different stitches in any one piece of work. In the colonial period flame stitch was used on pocket books and chair covers and tent stitch (needlepoint) was employed for pictures and screens, as well as those stitches which are usually associated with the term crewel embroidery.

Indian palampores were exported to Europe and floral designs from them found their way into crewel embroidery. Other patterns were taken from illuminated manuscrips, botany books and engravings, some of which were copies of earlier German and Italian publications. The patterns woven into Chinese silk also proved a source of inspiration to the embroideress.

Most eighteenth-century needlewomen used the carnation,

grapes, acanthus leaf, pomegranate and rose, the Tudor rose from England becoming the Whig rose in America. A little running stag is often shewn in crewel work. It represents the soul flying from the powers of evil which are represented by pursuing hounds.

Crewel embroidery was mainly polychrome, using shades of blue, pink, green, and all shades of yellow, gold and brown, and of course white. During the first half of the eighteenth century advertisements frequently appeared in newspapers in Boston, New York and Philadelphia for canvas and shaded crewels which had just arrived from London. Work in these areas was more sophisticated than that from rural areas where designs were simpler but the embroidery was just as forceful and as beautiful.

By the middle of the eighteenth century some embroidery was being done only in shades of blue, possibly inspired by the 'blue canton' chinaware brought back from the east by American sailors. A more likely explanation, however, may be that at this time instead of wool yarns more cotton and linen yarns began to be used and they did not take vegetable dyes, with the exception of indigo, very well.

The ground fabric of early crewel embroidery was fustian, a linen warp with a cotton weft in a twill weave, but later a plain woven linen ground was used.

Independence marked the beginning of the end of the great era of crewel embroidery. Fashions and styles in furniture were changing; silks were being imported from the east and hand embroidered bed hangings became old fashioned. Many of the bed hangings were cut down and made into coverlets which were sometimes quilted.

From 1830 until 1870 the coarser Berlin woolwork, using thicker yarns and harsh chemical dyes, superseded crewel embroidery. However, in 1898 two women in Deerfield, Massachusets began to make what became known as the 'Deerfield blue and white' embroidery. They used traditional crewel embroidery designs which were worked on a white linen ground in a blue linen or cotton thread.

Netting

The origins of netting go back further than one can trace but nets have been used over the centuries by fishermen, farmers and hunters among others. The use of decorative netting probably came to Europe from the east where veils of gold and silver mesh were worn by many women. In America and Britain wig makers used a netted mesh for the caul or foundation of their wigs and hairpieces. Netting was very popular in eighteenth- and nineteenth-century America and was one of the crafts included in the needlework teaching of the early finishing schools.

The Eskimo women in Alaska made intricate meshes in netting, and the ivory and bone needles they used were often carved by the men into whales and other symbolic shapes which they hoped would bring them luck on their fishing expeditions.

In America netting was used mostly for decorative fringes on bed and table furnishings and for trimming children's dresses. Martha Washington netted extensively. When heavy bed hangings were no longer required to shut out draughts and cold, many women were not able to obtain light draperies, so netted canopies were used as a substitute. The patterns used by the colonial women were usually combinations of geometric forms which created a lacey effect. Often tassels were added. Netted purses and costume accessories were made with fine silks.

Only two simple tools are needed for netting: the netting needle, round which the yarn is wound, and the mesh stick, which, according to its width, makes the size of the mesh. The foundation loop into which the first row of meshes is worked must be firm, and in the eighteenth century was attached to a lead-weighted cushion or a specially made netting box.

Indian Crafts

Indian tribes decorated their clothing and possessions long before the white settlers produced their brightly coloured glass trade beads. Decoration was mainly on skins and birch bark since cloth was not manufactured, except in the south west where the Navajo became famous for the woven blankets. The earliest form of decoration is thought to have been porcupine quillwork which was well established by the time the first white men reached America. The oldest piece of quillwork is on a pair of moccasins found in Utah, perhaps left there by an Athabascan at the time of the southward migration which took place between 1000 and 1500 A.D.

Indian 'beads' were also used to adorn skins and birch bark and were made of the native mineral substances of each area. These might include copper, soapstone, turquoise, seeds, shells, and the horns, teeth and claws of animals.

George Catlin, who observed and painted many Indians, commented on one small group he met on a trip through the southern Plains in 1835: 'The four women, dressed much alike, are clad in dresses of deer and elk skins, most curiously and elaborately garnished, and ornamented with porcupine quill work and beads....'

Wampum, white and purple beads made from clam shells, was in use on the eastern seaboard before the coming of the white man, and decorated the presentation belts made by the Iroquois tribe. A wampum belt would be given as a lasting symbol of an agreement between tribes of the north-east. They became important documentary evidence of treaties, including some connected with the founding of Pennsylvania by William Penn. Later wampum was used as currency and became legal tender in New Amsterdam.

Moose hair was used by Indians to adorn dress and household effects, sometimes plaited round a foundation of sinew, or with the hairs bunched together, the little bundles then being sewn to the skins with decorative stitches. Tradition has it that Ursuline nuns who came to Canada in the early seventeenth century were taught to use moose hair for embroidery by three English women who had been captured by Indians and who later became nuns. Silk was expensive and not easy to come by, and the short moose hair fibres which took a good dye made an effective substitute. By the end of the seventeenth century, the nuns, who lived near the site of present day Quebec, had begun to teach Huron women European type embroidery, and like beads and moosehair, fine cotton yarns became recognized as a natural Indian embroidery medium.

In the Great Lakes area trade goods such as woven cloth and silk ribbons, as well as sewing needles, thread and beads, were obtained by the Indians in exchange for furs. The ribbons were used with great effect in the silk appliqué patterns on shawls and other articles of clothing.

Navajo Blankets

The Navajo Indians came to the south-western deserts of America from Canada and Alaska. They were originally hunters and gatherers, but their ability to absorb new elements into their culture helped them to survive and become the largest tribe in America today. From their neighbours the Pueblos, who were farmers and grew among other things both brown and white varieties of cotton, the Navajo learnt the art of weaving, and with the introduction by the Spanish of sheep and horses they became semi-nomadic shepherds.

The 'churro' sheep of the Spanish peasants were introduced into America about 1540. The scrawny and long-legged animals were hardy, and their long brown wool required little preparation for spinning. Later Merino sheep were imported and cross-bred with the 'churros'. Thus in addition to the locally grown cotton, wool was introduced into the Pueblo looms, and the Navajos were quick to learn the weaver's art. They became known for their blankets, which were always simple in design with patterns based mainly on stripes.

The economic importance of textile production was realized by the Navajos, who found that they could trade their blankets to other tribes. One of the best known types of Navajo blanket is the 'chief pattern' blanket, which differs from all other types in that the warp runs the width rather than the length of the weaving.

There were no chiefs in the strict sense in the Navajo tribes and this type of blanket could have been worn by any member. Because they were extremely well made, however, the ownership of a 'chief pattern' blanket usually indicated that the wearer was a person of importance.

The development of the 'chief pattern' blanket can be divided into three main categories, although there are distinct variations within each of the three stages of development.

In the first phase the design consisted only of stripes, the earliest having narrow alternating bands of white and natural black-brown. As time passed there was a consistent broadening of the dark and light stripes and then symmetrically placed indigo blue stripes came to be included at the centre and at each end of the blanket. These first phase 'chief pattern' blankets have very narrow stripes of red used to outline the edge between the indigo and the main stripes.

In the second phase, nine rectangular blocks were inserted within the striped grid to make a balanced design. Dark brown stripes contrast with white, and rich indigo blue stripes are defined by thin red bands.

In the third phase the blocks evolved into a diamond motif, and by the 1870's the 'chief pattern' blanket had developed into a balanced combination of stripes and diamonds. In this phase there is a central full diamond, sometimes broken by the centre stripe, which is surrounded by eight triangular units at the edges.

During the second quarter of the nineteenth century a very ornate type of blanket known as the 'bayeta serape' began to be made. It is possible that they were made as special items to trade with the Spaniards and to be worn to mark an honoured position in the tribe. The most outstanding examples were made 'poncho' style with an opening in the middle, instead of the blanket being draped round the body as in the 'chief pattern' style. Navajo blankets are meant to be worn, therefore the design relates to the body. When the 'chief pattern' blanket is worn a complete diamond is seen centred on the front and on the back of the wearer.

The Navajos discovered plants and minerals with which to

dye the native black and white wool. Prickly pear, juniper, lichen, sumac, wild walnut, sage brush and other desert plants were used as well as mountain mahogany, root bark and pitch taken from the pinon (pinus edulus). However, the Navajo were unable to get a good red dye so they used the yarn from the bayeta. Bayeta was a wool cloth known in England as baize, and was originally made in Manchester and shipped via Spain to Mexico, whence it was brought into the south-west. Its threads were easily unravelled and spun into yarn. By the late nineteenth century American flannel was used, as well as the aniline dyes and machine-made yarns.

Colour has always meant a great deal to the Indian. Red is a favourite, symbolizing warmth, life and protection; white is symbolic of the rising sun, of life itself; blue, the south, a cloudless sky, peace; yellow, the west, sunset and deeds accomplished; black, north, clouds and cold.

The weaving of the Navajo blankets was done by the women of the tribes unlike the Pueblos whose men were the weavers. Although a lengthy process, weaving was very much a spare time activity. The loom was of a simple vertical construction which helps to explain the tendency towards horizontal striped and geometric designs. (see illustration 12). A simple flat single face technique was used. The old Navajo had no measurements, blankets being so many 'hand lengths' in size. There were no set patterns, each weaver carrying her design in her head. Preliminary drawings were never made. Two figures feature in many Navajo legends – Spider Man and Spider Woman. A Navajo baby girl was prepared for her future role as a weaver by having a spider's web rubbed on her hand and arm so that, according to Spider Man, when she grew up her fingers and arms would not tire from weaving. Spider Woman was supposed to have taught Navajo women how to weave on a loom which Spider Man had told them

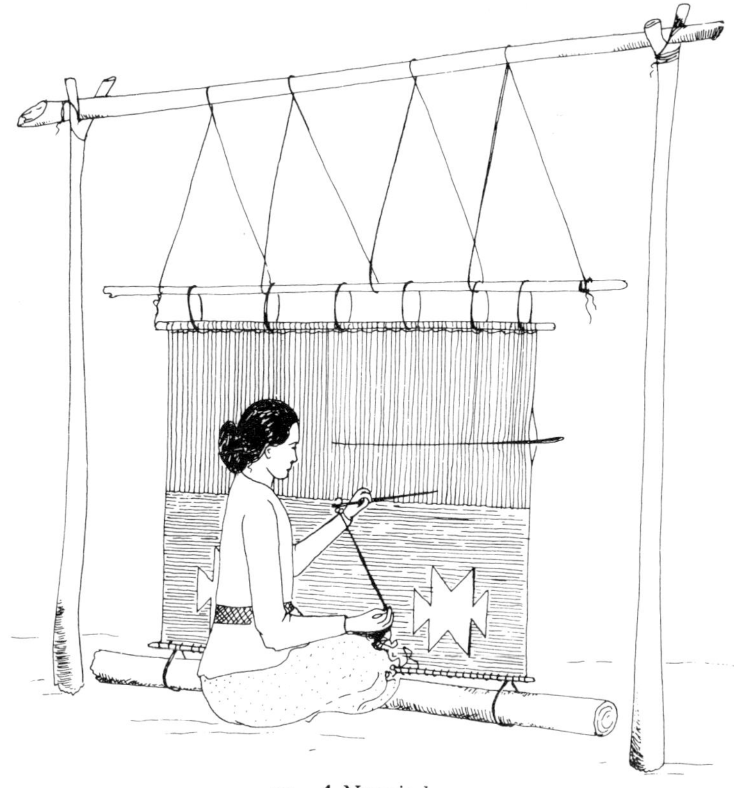

12. *A Navajo loom.*

how to make. The crosspoles were made of sky and earth cords, the warp sticks of sun rays, the healds of rock crystal and sheet lightning. The batten was a sun halo, white shell made the comb. There were four spindles: one a stick of zig zag lightning with a whorl of cannel coal; one a stick of flash lightning with a whorl of turquoise; a third had a stick of sheet lightning with a whorl of abalone; a rain streamer formed the stick of the fourth, and its whorl was white shell. After the Civil War the south-west was flooded with inferior

Yei

Bayeta Serape

Chief pattern
Phase 1.

13. *Navajo rugs.*

machine-made blankets. They were cheap and the Navajo weavers could not compete with them. However about this time certain traders began to suggest that Navajo blankets should be used as floor rugs and happily, after several reversals of fortune, there is now a great demand for Navajo rugs.

Regional differences today may be determined by style, pattern and colour. From the Two Grey Hills area come the finest of all rugs. Within a black border yarns of natural colours are blended to produce greys and browns which are used in a geometric pattern. Intensive carding is necessary to produce a high thread count, up to 110 wefts per inch, as for cashmere, instead of the more usual 30–50 wefts per inch. In contrast, the designs for the Yei rugs from the Shiprock area which were developed at the turn of the century, were taken from sand paintings, and although the Yei is a religious figure, the rugs had no religious significance. The figures were very colourful, and were displayed on a white background with a rainbow figure woven down two sides and across the bottom. These rugs were often used as wall hangings. The Ganado type rug was created by Juan Lorenzo Hubbell who ran a trading post there from 1878 to 1930. Ganado rugs have a strong geometric design using greys, whites and black on a red aniline dyed background. From Crystal comes one of the most distinctive of all Navajo styles. Bands of solid colour alternate with 'zig zag' panels using two or three wefts of contrasting colour. There is no border and only vegetable dyes are used.

The demand for rugs far exceeds supply as weaving is a time consuming occupation. The Navajo, however, have been able to adapt to modern requirements, and it could be said that their skill and adaptability as weavers have helped them to survive where other tribes have perished.

Quill Work

Porcupine quill embroidery was carried on mainly in the Northern Woodlands and Great Lakes areas, a vast tract of land which covered most of Canada and much of the United States east of the Mississippi. Work from different areas may be identified by variations in design, colours and stitches used in sewing. It is a decoration which adds life and colour to any surface to which it is attached.

There is a feeling of lightness in all woodlands art; the scroll and double curve motif were very typical of woodlands style as were leaf and floral motifs. Later beadwork preserved these old patterns which were extended to include the geometric. The use of trade materials such as beads, silver, ribbon applique and commercial yarns helped to develop the more elaborate European inspired patterns.

The Micmac Indians of eastern Canada made a speciality of decorating birchbark boxes with quill work. Their style was graceful but not so exact as that of the Cree who made a great deal of excellent quill work before 1850. Much quill work was made during times of peace for early colonists and brought back to England and Scotland, sometimes by serving soldiers. The Micmac used a wide variety of shapes and excelled at changes of colour.

The early nineteenth-century Plains quill work was influenced by the Woodlands patterns but soon became bolder and more striking to look at. Early Plains quill work used colours such as cream, orange, brown, and black. To these colours were later added red, green and blue. By the end of the nineteenth century very bright colours were being used.

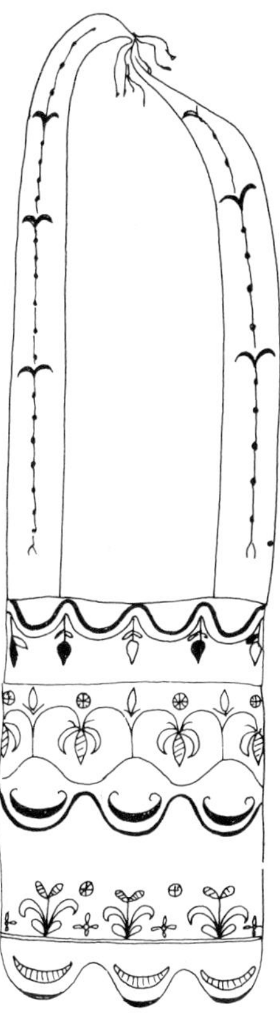
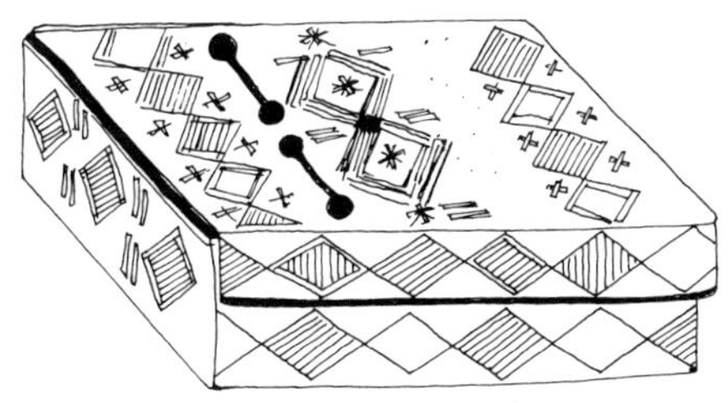

14. *Quillwork on a Crow Indian child's costume, an old birch bark box from the North East Woodlands (note the uneven pattern), and an Iroquois bag.*

In addition to using quills to decorate boxes and clothing the Sioux quilled medicine bundles and cradle boards.

The quills could be wrapped, netted, sewn, chained, spliced or plaited. When sewing quills on to hides a thin strip of sinew was used for thread, the end being twisted into a sharp point. The upper surface of the hide was perforated with the point of a chipped stone to allow the thread to be pushed through and carried in small 'back stitches' over the quills, which closely overlapped. The quills penetrated only the upper layer of the hide. The Indian women held the quills in their mouths, softening them and making them more flexible while they were sewing. The patterns were marked out with a sharp pointed awl when the skin was stretched taut.

In the Great Lakes region the porcupine quill work done on birch bark was not sewn, but pushed into holes made with an awl. The bark then contracted and held them in place. As time went on the birch bark was covered with cloth which was then embroidered with quills.

Beadwork

It is said that everything the Indian made he decorated, and with the introduction of glass trade beads into America this tradition received fresh impetus. The early Spanish explorers in the south-west, the Russian traders in the north-west, and the English and Dutch settlers who came to the east coast all brought trade beads to exchange for horses, food and furs. The Hudson's Bay Company and other fur trading companies, were responsible for spreading them among the Indians as their trappers travelled westwards into the wilderness. By about 1800 bead work was fairly well established in north America. Beads were becoming standardized and were sold in the form of hanks, each being made up of five or six strings. In the fur trading areas hanks were valued at a certain number of animal skins.

In 1900 the Pima Indians would give thirty of the beautiful blue 'padre' beads for a good horse and on one occasion the U.S. Army paid the Mohave Indians six pounds of white beads, among other things, as a ransom for a girl whom they had captured.

Early glass trade beads made in Venice were too large for sewn bead work and were used mainly for necklaces. These were followed in the late seventeenth century by 'pony' beads, about one-eighth to one-tenth of an inch in diameter and roughly shaped. They were blue, white and black and called 'pony' beads because the first traders used ponies to carry the beads to the Indians. It was not until about 1800 that they reached the Plains area. Later came the tiny many-coloured 'cut' beads, and then the 'seed' beads which were of a more uniform size and were used for loom weaving, and for working

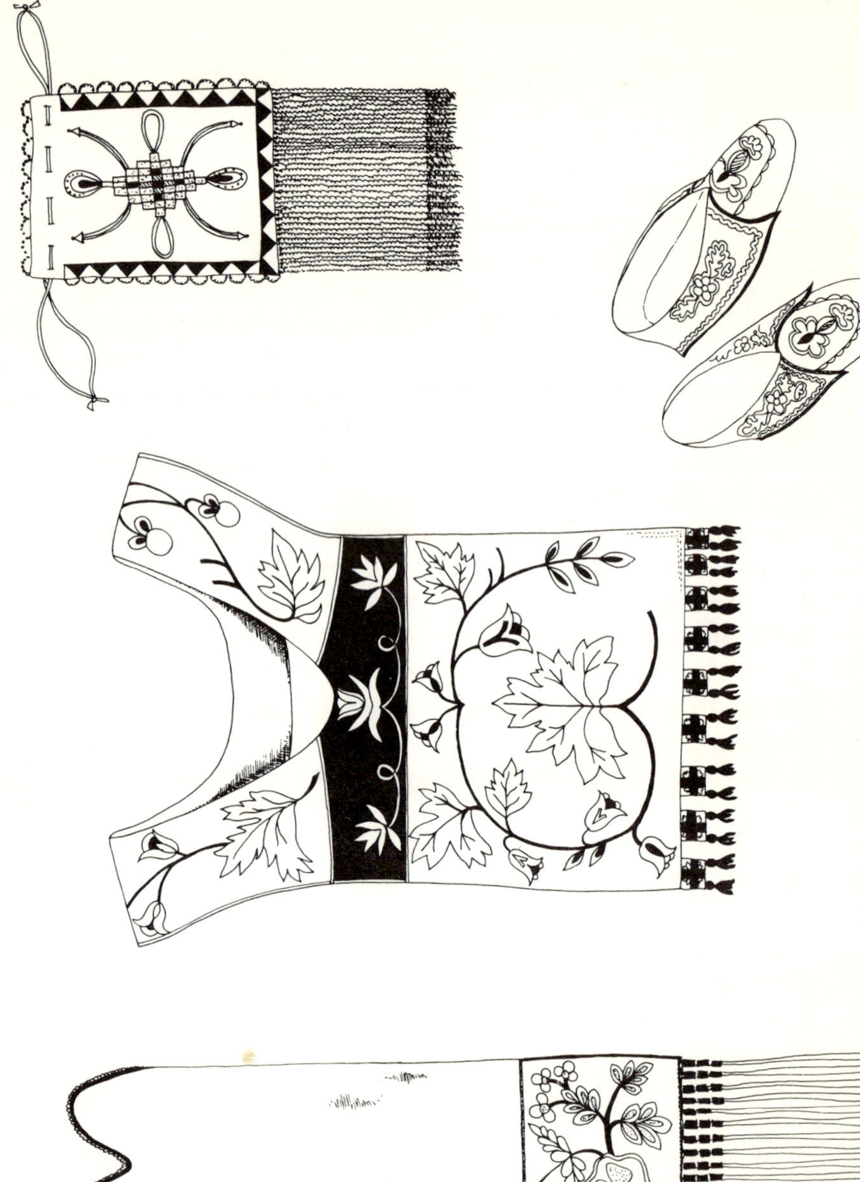

15. *Beadwork on a pipe bag and a shoulder bag from the Great Lakes area, a smaller bag from the Plains region, and moccasins from the Eastern Woodlands.*

on buckskin and cloth. Seed beads were in use in the east from the early 1700's but did not reach the south-west until the middle of the nineteenth century. The 'padre' bead was an opaque sky blue glass bead with a satin like finish, and it is thought to be one of the earliest trade beads in the south-west. It is possible that they may have been traded by Coronado himself.

In spite of some general similarities between the patterns used by the different tribes of the Plains, the decorative work of each area was distinctive. On the northern Plains for example the western Sioux developed abstract designs of triangles, squares and stepped lines against a background of blue or white beads. Further west the Blackfoot decorated their war shirts with bold checked patterns, while the Kiowa and Comanche used bands of green, yellow and red beading for borders. The Cheyenne also specialized in beadwork borders, mainly of blue, black and white. After 1875 some of the finest beadwork was done by the Crow and Blackfoot Indians. The Blackfoot specialized in dresses and capes with contrasting bands of beadwork from shoulder to shoulder. The Crow decorated horse trappings with lines of white beads against blue, yellow, red, and green geometric shapes. The Penobscot Indians of Maine made beadwork cuffs and are still making them at the present time. The importation of trade goods and the interchange of patterns between tribes helped to produce changes in colour and design.

As well as regional differences in design, there are also colour variations. Glass trade beads came in a variety of bright colours, but the Iroquois and other eastern woodland tribes were famous for their use of the small white seed beads on broadcloth. They were applied to the cloth in fine scroll designs, and were often found as border patterns on leggings, robes and women's costumes. Colour was sometimes introduced by running silk ribbons under the beads. This Victorian inspired beadwork of the late nineteenth century was made for sale to the tourist.

Beadwork was primarily a woman's craft. There were two methods of working beads: by sewing and by weaving on a loom. Woven beadwork began in the late 1700's and was done by the tribes of the Great Lakes region with a small loom or a needle. Sewn beadwork is carried out by two main methods: the lazy stitch done by the tribes of the central and southern Plains, and the 'spot' or 'overlay' stitch employed by the tribes of the northern United States and Canada. Both are derived from the methods of sewing porcupine quills.

For 'lazy' stitch the beads are threaded on to a length of yarn which is then secured to the skin or cloth. Work done by this method has a ridged appearance. The designs appear to be raised and can be padded. The 'overlay' stitch is worked by threading beads, and with another needle and thread, catching down the yarn between every few beads, as in couching. By this method the curves which are so necessary for the floral patterns can be worked.

Baskets and Birchbark

Indian tribes noted for the making of baskets were the Pomo who lived on the Californian coast, and the Pima and Papago who lived on the border between Arizona and New Mexico. Baskets could be made in two ways – either woven or coiled, from natural fibres such as straw, willow, grass or yucca.

The Pomo embroidered feathers on the baskets which were presented to friends or given as wedding gifts. By an optical illusion the arrow patterns on Pomo baskets seem to turn into trees, and the diamond pattern which is common to most central Californian baskets, suggests a snake.

The Pima made shallow baskets or trays for gathering food, mainly mesquite beans, while the Apache made large storage baskets for holding grain. The western Apache made burden baskets as gifts or for use as food baskets as well as for their primary function of carrying.

Basketry gambling trays with a design of humans joining hands were made by the Yokut Indians. These trays were used for a dice game played by the women. The dice were made of half shells of walnut or acorn filled with pitch and studded with abalone shell.

The Modoc tribe of northern California added red wool embroidery, at which they excelled, to brighten their baskets.

In addition to looking very attractive birchbark is also waterproof and fire resistant. It can be stitched, rolled, bent or engraved. When peeled it is fawn in colour, is soft and flexible and has a pink inner layer. Birchbark can be used to make roof mats, boxes and containers of all kinds.

To make patterns and silhouettes on the sides of containers the inner layer was scraped away leaving the pattern in relief.

The Ojibway Midewiwin scrolls were made of birchbark and had lines and symbols cut into the bark. The scrolls were used for several purposes but mainly for discussion and the interpretation of the ritual by the Mide priests. The circle represents the world and it is guarded by four spirits which represent the four directions.

The Mohegan Indians made and still make splint baskets of birch bark, decorated with patterns which have been cut into the flat surface of a potato which is then dipped into paint.

Suggested Reading

American Needlework, Georgiana B. Harbeson. Bonanza Books, New York.

Homespun and Blue, Martha Genung Stearns. Charles Scribners' Sons, New York.

The Art of Crewel Embroidery, Mildred J. Davis. Crown Publishers Inc., New York.

American Crewelwork, Mary Taylor Landon and Susan Burrows Swan. Macmillan.

Patchwork, Averil Colby. Batsford.

Quilting, Averil Colby. Batsford.

Quilts in America, Myron and Patsy Orlofsky. McGraw Hill, 1975.

The Pieced Quilt – an American Design Tradition, Jonathan Holstein. New York Graphic Society Ltd., Greenwich, Conn., 1973.

The Perfect Patchwork Primer, Beth Gutcheon. Penguin.

Old Patchwork Quilts, Ruth Finley. Bell.

The Standard Book of Quiltmaking, Marguerite Ickis. Dover.

Keep Me Warm One Night – Woven coverlets in Eastern Canada, Harold and Dorothy Burnham. University of Toronto Press and the Royal Ontario Museum, 1972.

A Book of Handwoven Coverlets, Eliza Calvert Hall. Little Brown and Co., 1914.

American Hooked and Sewn Rugs, Folk Art Underfoot, Joel and Kate Kopp. Dutton, 1975.

Iroquois Crafts, Carrie A. Lyford. Bureau of Indian Affairs.

Southwestern Arts and Crafts, Tom Bahti. K. C. Publications, Flagstaff, Arizona.

Navajo Weaving, its Technique and History, Charles A. Amsden. Reprinted, 1972.

Navajo Rugs, Past Present and Future, Gilbert S. Maxwell. Desert-South west Publications, 1963.

THE AMERICAN MUSEUM IN BRITAIN tells the story of how Americans lived from the seventeenth to the nineteenth centuries through a series of completely furnished rooms with original panelling brought from the United States and installed in Claverton Manor. Contrasts in the life of colonial New England are shown in the Puritan Keeping Room of the 1680's and the cosy tavern kitchen of the 1770's with its beehive oven and well-protected bar, in the blue-green panelled living room from Lee, New Hampshire and the mid-eighteenth-century parlour of Captain Perley who led his Minute Men at the battle of Bunker Hill. The sophistication of the parlours from Colchester, Connecticut and Baltimore, Maryland, introduces the period of the New Republic. An early nineteenth-century country style bedroom contrasts with the elegance of the Greek Revival dining room of New York and the richly ornate bedroom from New Orleans at the time of the Civil War.

In addition there are galleries devoted to the American Indian, the Pennsylvania Dutch, the religious community of the Shakers, and the isolated Spanish colonists of New Mexico. There are further exhibits on the Opening of the West, whaling (with a Captain's cabin reproduced from the last of the great Yankee whalers), textiles (with a fine collection of quilts and hooked rugs), pewter, glass, and silver. In the attractive grounds is the semicircular gallery displaying the vigorous forms and primitive designs of American Folk Art. There is also an 1830 Conestoga wagon, the observation platform of a railroad car, and a replica of a Cheyenne tepee.

Public opening: April to mid-October, daily (Mondays excepted), 2 pm–5 pm.

The Museum is open to schools throughout the year (January excepted) at the following times:

Mid-October to March	Monday to Friday	9.30 am–12.30 pm 2.00 pm–5.00 pm
April to mid-October	Mondays	As above
	Tuesday to Friday	Mornings only

The John Judkyn Memorial, Freshford Manor, Bath, is associated with the Museum and provides a loan service of material relating to American history and culture. Some loan kits can be seen at the Museum, and information on borrowing is provided.

All enquiries concerning these educational services should be made to:

The Education Department,
The American Museum in Britain,
Claverton Manor,
Bath — Tel: Bath 60503.